Storm Chasers

Storm Chasers

30 Days to Lock Down on Hope in the Middle of a Storm Surge

WENDY AGUIAR

CREDENCE
HOUSE
PRESS

First Edition

Cover original art painting by Laura Martin
Cover layout and design by Shelley Savoy

ISBN: 978-1-7350956-0-8 (paperback)
ISBN: 978-1-7350956-1-5 (e-book)

Published by Credence House Press
credencehousepress.com

Some storms are predictable; others are not. Most people can relate to the feeling of utter helplessness and fear when the storms of life catch us by surprise. This practical devotional contains original musings, poems and songs to remind you that you are never alone. This is your 30-day journey to hope. Nothing catches our Lord by surprise; in fact, God lives in the eye of the storm and so should you!

Dedication

To Valerie, my one and only sister. Though you are no longer here to brag on your "baby sister," I know that you are watching from Heaven and coercing angels into reading my first book. Your remarkable wit and talent always inspired me, in spite of the many storms you faced in life. Amid the chaos, we always loved each other. Those who knew you best realized that you were a prolific and eloquent writer who truly deserved to be published. This book is for you.

To every person who has ever caused a storm in my life, THANK YOU. Without your contribution, I would never know the beauty and serenity of a clear day. God never allows pain to be wasted. You have given me the gift of experience-a true boon for any budding author!

To the storm dwellers, you have not been abandoned. A calm breeze may have become a threatening gale; as darkness fades, turn your face towards the rising sun because THE SON loves you with abandon. You can find hope through Christ, even in the middle of a storm surge.

Contents

Acknowledgments

In the Bible, there is an impactful story about Jesus healing the ten lepers. Only one returned to give thanks. I never want to fail to show appreciation for the people who have blessed my life. Without the friends who hold me accountable and set a great example, I would be forever dreaming of writing a book without ever putting pen to paper. A project like this is not possible without loved ones who understand what it takes for productivity to occur. Occasionally, that means unreturned phone calls and long hours in "the zone." Thank you to everyone who loves me enough to understand the meaning of my solitude. I am forever grateful.

Storms in life are inevitable, but the people who help us through them should never be taken for granted. First, thank you to my Savior for being the best storm navigator throughout every moment of my crazy life. Without You, life becomes an exercise in futility.

Corbin, I want to thank you for being my inspiration to write many of these devotionals. You are a complex, brilliant and amazing person. It is an honor to be your mother. I will always love you dearly and pray God's best for your future. Your writing is second to none and I thank you for the feedback you gave me when I texted or knocked on your door with another crazy idea. I can always count on you for brutal honesty, and even when I dislike it, I still respect you for it in the end. As you embrace your adulthood, please know that I am proud of you.

Thank you to my entire family, but without parents, there would be no book. Dad, you are an amazing writer and I will never forget how I felt whenever you sent me one of your editorial letters printed in *The Miami Herald*. That motivated me to reach higher and dig deeper within myself to chase my own dreams. I hope that you will continue chasing yours. I love you! Mercy, you always have something positive to say about my goals in life. Your funny texts brought a smile to my face when I desperately needed a little break from writing. Mom, you raised me as a single parent, which is not an easy task. I remember the way you would crumple up my homework assignments that were not well-written, challenging me to get it right; in doing so, you taught me that mediocrity is not acceptable. Thank you for the delicious sustenance during my long hours at the computer. No one holds a candle to you when it comes to cooking skills. I would still be a starving writer if you hadn't staged those culinary interventions.

Laura, thank you for lending me that incredible talent for my book cover design.

James, thank you for always cheering me on and for being supportive of my dreams. You pray for me and encourage me to believe in myself. Through the many storms you have personally encountered, I have never seen you demonstrate a resentful attitude towards others. I may not say it often, but this makes me want to be a better person. Thank you for picking up the phone and letting me bounce my writing ideas off you and for giving me perspective when things don't go according to plan. I appreciate your gentle spirit, even when mine is stormy. I love you.

If friends are gems in the crown of life, God has truly blessed me with a crown of the highest value. My circle of close friends may be small, but I cherish the quality people who walk through the storms of life with me. I don't need an exhausting social circle, just a few divine connections.

Shawna, you are my best friend on this side of Heaven. Thank you for encouraging me to be the best version of myself and for setting the bar high in your own life. I value every childhood memory and those moments build a lifetime of memories that shape me as a person and as a writer. I love you and respect you more than words could ever express.

Octavio and Trudy, you have been steadfast and supportive for as long as I can remember. I value our friendship and the advice you have offered during the storms in my life. Your home was my refuge during many hurricanes, but we made it (and you helped me to pick up the pieces when I returned home to survey the damage). Octavio, thank you for allowing me to include your miraculous healing story in this book. Trudy, thank you for reminding me to cling to God during the storms instead of going on a shopping spree that I would regret later.

Pam, my close friend and teaching mentor, thank you from the bottom of my heart. Your wisdom and love have been instrumental in shaping my career. Thanks for the pep talks and for holding me accountable when I make excuses for inaction. Your eagle eye was a blessing as I embarked on this new territory. Even though I can't repay you for this labor of love, God sees every moment you spent pouring over my emails and He will surely reward you.

Linda, I have watched you weather the storms of life as a champion. You are a fun travel companion and a great spiritual mom. If you hadn't agreed to take a road trip to Bradenton with me, I might have still been stuck in a rut with no book written. God knew how much we both needed a short retreat to refresh our spirits after enduring some personal storms.

Reneyda, your contagious smile, acceptance, lovely garden and hospitality made a difference. The laughter and spontaneity energized me enough to tackle this writing project and I am eternally grateful.

Kechi, you have been not only a wonderful colleague, but also a good friend. What I appreciate about you is that you confront me with truth. There have been times in my life when I chose not to prepare for the storm, and you didn't sugar coat the situation. You always have fresh insights and philosophical truths that linger in my mind long after we say goodbye. Above all, your encouragement and motivation have made a difference. God knew how much I needed that. To write this book, I had to become uncomfortable with my status quo. A million thanks!

Pastor Darrell, the drive-through prayers and words of encouragement gave me the spiritual shove I needed to cross the finish line for this book when I became weary. God bless you.

Mike and Elizabeth Shreve, thank you for building a spiritual foundation in my life through your ministry and covenant friendship. In Bradenton, the sermon, "Inheritors of the Mountain" helped to reawaken my stagnant vision to write a book. I have seen you both weather many storms with authenticity and character. Thank you for demonstrating integrity for me.

Introduction

Eagles. Their keen instinctive awareness alerts them when a storm is approaching. Audacity. They embrace the situation instead of avoiding the bad weather. This majestic bird ascends even higher, almost daring the breeze to reach hurricane strength. Eagles have a fortunate wing design that allows them to soar even higher in an updraft, rarely flapping their wings. The picture I want to paint for you today is one of total surrender. The eagle does not waste any of its energy fighting against the storm, instead, it comes into alignment with the fiercest winds and uses them to gain altitude; this is the key to serenity. There is purpose in the turbulence. God lives in the eye of the storm and His peace surrounds us when we center our lives completely around Him.

This book has been brewing in my spirit for a long time. I did not know the title or the exact format, but I did know one thing: God never allows our pain to be wasted. So often, I wondered where God was during my darkest moments. Perhaps you can relate. I came from a broken home and I know the pain of dysfunctional relationships and betrayal. Storms may come from unexpected places or they may surface as distracting bumps along the road of life, but we have a solid anchor. God had never left me, but I had to realize that storms were purposeful. We do not always encounter storms because of disobedience or some misstep that disappointed God. We simply live in a flawed world. The writing for this devotional occurred against the backdrop of a global pandemic, the likes of which this generation has never known. Two months ago, this chaos was unthinkable. The sun was shining with no visible clouds; blissful complacency was everywhere. Fast forward to total lockdown and a palpable atmosphere of panic and isolation.

Here is my promise to every reader: This devotional will give you hope and some practical tactics for dealing with adversity. The devil isn't in the details. God is. I challenge you to connect with your storm and learn something new through the process. I started this book after returning from the west coast of Florida. My short retreat had already been paid for and the stress in my life had reached a boiling point. This road trip was my mental health break. With my sanitation arsenal packed and Psalm 91 quoted, I braved the unknown with a recently widowed friend. Closures were just beginning to occur and lockdown measures were imminent, having already begun in southeast Florida. I was in desperate need of some respite, but storms can chase us anywhere. The day after we arrived, lovely Siesta Key Beach closed and restaurants bade us farewell, and yet that time with God was priceless. The seeds for this book germinated through a stormy season. God lives in the eye of your storm, so I challenge you to become a storm chaser!

DAY # 1

God Lives in the Eye of the Storm

Living in South Florida has its drawbacks. As a lifetime resident, I have witnessed hurricane evacuations become the annoying order of the day. Such is the price for living in paradise. (O.K. paradise is a stretch.) But last year was another busy hurricane season. As my son and I evacuated and went to stay with some friends who live in a more substantial dwelling, I noticed how contagious emotions could be. Normally benign citizens prepared to do battle at the local grocery stores and gas stations as lines stretched for blocks. I digress. My friends were well prepared for Hurricane Wilma. From the first gust of wind, it was obvious that we had a long and noisy evening ahead of us. During the night, sleep evaded us all as we crowded around the radio by candlelight with the standard hurricane fare of chips, cookies and other foods forbidden by health gurus. The wind whipped against the house turning roof tiles into projectiles and garbage can lids into Frisbees. Torrential rain and wind continued for about an hour as I held my son safe in my arms. Then, complete silence ensued. The radio update informed us that the eye of the storm was directly over our local area but cautioned against going outside because of difficulty in predicting exactly when the eye would pass over and the backlash of the storm would begin.

The back patio, which is partially enclosed, seemed like a logical place from which to observe. The calm was almost eerie as not even a leaf was rustling. In fact, judging by the conditions, it was easy to forget that a storm was ever in the vicinity. In the stillness, I felt completely safe and at ease. The sky was perfect and the stars shone clearly. Suddenly, a howling intensified gust ripped around the house and destroyed my reverie as I frantically made my way indoors before a large tree toppled nearby. The worst part of the storm began and continued until dawn. The eye of the storm always contains the calmest weather and is a safe place as long as you know its exact dimensions. To be sure, the eye functions as the only stabilizing force in a hurricane. Likewise, God is our safety and our constant in the center of the turmoil and instability that threatens to overwhelm our lives. As long as we stay directly situated in the center of His will, we dwell safely while destruction rages on all sides of us. In the stillness, He speaks to us. Yet if we step outside of the parameters that He sets for us, the winds and rain can wreak havoc on our lives. The eye of a physical storm is always larger in dimension at the top and smaller at the bottom. Spiritually, as we move upward in our relationship with the Lord, we have greater peace; yet in the absence of communion with God, storms begin to close in on us and we wonder where God is. The fact remains that He never relocated. He lives in the eye of the storm and that is the safest place to be.

Daily Readings

*"I will lie down and sleep in peace, for you alone,
O Lord, make me dwell in safety."*

— Psalms 4:8 (NIV) —

*"He who dwells in the shelter of the Most High
will rest in the shadow of the Almighty."
I will say of the Lord, "He is my refuge and
my fortress, my God, in whom I trust." …
"A thousand may fall at your side, ten thousand
at your right hand, but it will not come near you."*

— Psalm 91:1-2 and 7 (NIV) —

DAY # 2

A Song for the Storm

The song, "With My Life" can be a simple reminder to give thanks in the middle of a storm. Sometimes, being thankful for the little things can make the storm bearable. In the middle of the coronavirus pandemic, be thankful for family, solitude, rest, health and provision. Yes, it is inconvenient, but praise will help you to win the battle. Thank Him in advance because this storm will eventually pass; for the moment, embrace the rare chance to set new priorities. Things don't matter. People do. Celebrate simplicity and tackle that project at home. Sing a song through this storm!

1. Lord, for every breath I breathe
   for all the joy I've known...

   The things some people take for granted
   all the love You've shown

   The tears You gently wipe away
   Surrender's sweet embrace

   I want to tell You thank you:
   for it's only by Your grace.

   Chorus
   From my heart, I give my greatest offering
   With my lips, I'll sing a song to You
   Yes, I could find a thousand ways
   to show how You're adored...
   But with my life, I'm saying "Thank You, Lord."

2. In every generation, Lord,
   Your Word remains the same

   The beacon to a distant shore
   for those who call Your name

   Oh that men would praise Your name
   for all the things You've done

   Though nine forget to come and thank You
   Let me be the one! (Back to Chorus)

Daily Reading

"Rejoice always, pray continually,
give thanks in all circumstances;
for this is God' s will for you in Christ Jesus."

— 1 THESSALONIANS 5:16-18 (NIV) —

DAY # 3

Vision in the Storm

This poem is called "Destiny Calls." It is important to stay focused on your vison and destiny when you are in a difficult place. Never allow the anxiety of the moment to cause you to forget God's eternal promises. Remember His word when the flood is rising!

God has planted in your heart
a very special seed.
A dream, a vision, something you must water
and must feed.
Something you should guard because
its value is so great.

Your destiny and purpose too
is not just chance or fate.
Young people forfeit destiny
because their years are few.
Old people feel they've lived too long
to have a work to do.
So many lives are lived in vain
when visions dim and fade
Never knowing how much impact
that they could have made.
A heart for nations! Reformation!
God knows your desire.
So fan the flame when doubts or people
would put out your fire.
You're so important in God's plan
with such a role to play.
Superstars aren't what He needs-
Just hearts that will obey.

Daily Reading

For the vision is yet for an appointed time, but at the end it shall speak, and not lie: though it tarry, wait for it; because it will surely come, it will not tarry.

— HABAKKUK 2:3 (KJV) —

DAY # 4

His Name in the Storm

The name of Jesus means so much.
Where can I begin?
Healing and salvation:
Freedom from the grip of sin.
A refuge and a fortress-
The rock on which we stand.
Our closest friend: The one who bears our scars
in His own hand.
Jesus means protection like no weapon can afford.
The mention of His name can shatter
any chain or cord.
His still small voice means comfort to a broken heart;

Yet at His roar the clouds roll back! Oceans move apart!
His name has changed the total course
of all humanity.
Upon this fact the most decided skeptics still agree.
No matter what the question is-
The answer's still the same-
For everything we'll ever need is found within
THAT NAME!

Daily Reading

³⁵ *That day when evening came, he said to his disciples, "Let us go over to the other side." ³⁶ Leaving the crowd behind, they took him along, just as he was, in the boat. There were also other boats with him. ³⁷ A furious squall came up, and the waves broke over the boat, so that it was nearly swamped. ³⁸ Jesus was in the stern, sleeping on a cushion. The disciples woke him and said to him, "Teacher, don't you care if we drown?"*

³⁹ *He got up, rebuked the wind and said to the waves, "Quiet! Be still!" Then the wind died down and it was completely calm.*

⁴⁰ *He said to his disciples, "Why are you so afraid? Do you still have no faith?"*

⁴¹ *They were terrified and asked each other, "Who is this? Even the wind and the waves obey him!"*

— MARK 4:35-41 (NIV) JESUS CALMS THE STORM —

DAY # 5

Vessels in the Storm

I pray that this poem touches your heart and reminds you to be the hands and feet of Jesus. There has been no greater time to make a difference than right now. Stop making excuses and reach out to someone today. It may be just one person who needs an encouraging word or act of kindness. Ask God to show you how to reach out. He has anointed and called you to be a light in your sphere of influence. We live in a society where selfishness and "me time" is normal. God occasionally rocks our boat with a storm to see if we are willing to have faith. Volunteer. Bless someone. Speak life. Carry a burden for someone who is too weak to carry their own. God promises to empower you!

God is calling out today for vessels
He can use: Looking high and low
For someone willing He will choose.
Not for style, personality, or even fame-
but precious saints who love to hear
the mention of His name.
Maybe He will find them in the roughest
part of town taking time with sin-sick souls
while other Christians frown.
Sometimes they go against the flow
or what their friends may feel
To follow Christ in such a way
that people see it's real.
The mandate has been given!
All vessels must be pure. Yielded to the potter.
Their testimony sure.
The fields are white to harvest.
Sincere vessels hear His plea-
As God asks, "Whom can I send?
Who will agree to go for Me?"

Daily Reading

¹⁴⁻¹⁷ Dear friends, do you think you'll get anywhere in this if you learn all the right words but never do anything? Does merely talking about faith indicate that a person really has it? For instance, you come upon an old friend dressed in rags and half-starved and say, "Good morning, friend! Be clothed in Christ! Be filled with the Holy Spirit!" and walk off without providing so much as a coat or a cup of soup—where does that get you? Isn't it obvious that God-talk without God-acts is outrageous nonsense?

— James 2:14-17 (MSG) (Faith in Action) —

DAY # 6

Preparing for the Storm

Storm prediction is an imperfect science. As such, people tend to dismiss warnings and wait until there is a more imminent threat before stocking up on supplies. Once a person actually goes through a storm and feels the impact, the urgency increases and annual preparation becomes a lifestyle. This is the case in South Florida and as a native Floridian, hurricane rituals are my unfortunate birthright. The obvious provisions include food, flashlights, batteries, water, (did I mention food?) and such. Many people prepare for hurricanes as a community and people may huddle together during a storm. These weather-related threats have a season with a specific beginning and ending; for that we are thankful. In some years, we emerge unscathed and devour those hurricane snacks!

Yet pandemics, such as the coronavirus, have caught us off guard. We have no modern frame of reference for anything this lethal or unpredictable. There is no supply list that covers every possible scenario because medical professionals as well as average citizens are on the same learning curve. The unknown is a scary place and this storm is changing rapidly. The good news is that God is omniscient; I am so grateful that His knowledge dwarfs human understanding. The anxiety is building as people wonder when this unprecedented storm will pass. Social distancing has caused many people to feel loneliness and despair. Suffering is much easier to manage when we know the ending point just as the light at the end of a tunnel brings hope and direction.

A storm is defined as a violent disturbance of the atmosphere. If anything qualifies as a storm, the coronavirus does. The global atmosphere is laden with anxiety, suspicion and frustration. And yet, God already outlines everything that we need to prepare for a storm. The coronavirus directives given by officials include standards of cleanliness, social distance, awareness, caution, and above all, willingness to sacrifice our will in order to put others first. These are good tips for any believer even in the best of times! This storm is not one in which we can gather strength from others; go to your mountain alone to pray. The preparation for this storm must be done internally.

Here is your ultimate lockdown list:

1. Confront things in your life that you may have avoided with the busy schedule.

2. Lock into your time with God and your family and tune out all distractions.

3. Resurrect a personal dream or vision that has been on the shelf.

4. Rediscover who you are and embrace the solitude. Ask God for direction.

Daily Reading

*The name of the LORD is a strong tower;
the righteous man runs into it and is safe.*

— Proverbs 18:10 (ESV) —

DAY # 7

Storm Chaser –
A Song of Trust

Storm chasing is broadly defined as the pursuit of severe weather conditions. I have always wondered why people would intentionally put themselves into harm's way. Perhaps the motive is curiosity, adventure, media coverage or scientific inquiry; the important thing is that instead of running from the dangerous situation, they stare it down and live each moment with abandon. In a literal sense, this would not be my idea of wisdom in daily life, however, I have to respect something about that sense of adventure and absolute trust

21

in a positive outcome. As human beings, storm chasers obviously experience fear, but it doesn't control their lives. In the Word of God, storms always served a purpose. Sometimes they were used to build faith, other times as judgment and still other times they resulted from a wrong decision. Regardless of the cause or purpose of a storm, we can learn to trust our God through every type of storm. I hope that the words of this song speak to your heart in the middle of turmoil.

1. Though storms come and the rain falls down
   Wind blows through the temple; hear me now.
   You are a beacon-Glory sweeps through
   Speak to me softly. Lord, I trust You.

2. Love like no other. You give me Your all.
   Safe from the darkness, I know I won't fall.
   Fire by night and a cloud by day.
   Plagues may surround me; show me the way.

Chorus
I dance to Your voice in the storm.
I hide in Your arms in the storm.
You walk on the waves of the storm.
Call me to You.
Call me to You.
(Repeat slowly 2X)

Daily Reading

²⁻⁴ Consider it a sheer gift, friends, when tests and challenges come at you from all sides. You know that under pressure, your faith-life is forced into the open and shows its true colors. So don't try to get out of anything prematurely. Let it do its work so you become mature and well-developed, not deficient in any way.

— JAMES 1:2-4 (MSG) FAITH UNDER PRESSURE —

DAY # 8

Storm Damage Assessment

After a storm, it is normal practice for a damage assessment to be conducted to determine whether or not a structure is still habitable. Let's take a look at each category of the typical FEMA damage assessment through spiritual eyes:

1. **Destroyed** – A destroyed residence is within imminent threat of collapse because the load-bearing walls are weakened. This happens when we trust in earthly things and allow the storms of life to destroy us instead of drawing closer to God. Weak foundations cause some to walk away from the Lord.

2. **Major** – When major damage occurs to a home, the foundation shifts and crumbles. Any storm that has a major impact on our lives affects our daily ability to function. We may be disappointed in God and go through a season of depression. Serious events shake us to our core and help us to reevaluate.

3. **Minor** – Homes with minor damage are still very habitable, albeit with repairs. In these cases, most of the damage is non-structural and has more to do with aesthetics and convenience. When storms only cause minimal disruption in our lives, we are grateful and more appreciative of the good times. Usually, encouragement from a friend, praise music and prayer will help us to reset.

4. **Inaccessible** – An inaccessible home has blocked access. This means that there is no way that a resident can reach the home safely. When we go through a storm, we sometimes put up roadblocks to protect ourselves from further hurt. Jesus desires to knock on the door of your heart, but a homeowner can display a sign that says "No Soliciting" and block further access. Don't allow the storms in your life to make your spirit inaccessible. Open up and allow Him to change you through this season and make you a better version of yourself.

5. **Affected** – Storms occasionally impact a home without causing disruption. Perhaps a porch, outer

structure or landscaping may suffer, but the home is still solid. Jesus never promises that we won't be affected by this imperfect world. We may sustain cuts and bruises, but He does always walk beside us!

Daily Reading

[24] "So then, anyone who hears these words of mine and obeys them is like a wise man who built his house on rock. [25] The rain poured down, the rivers flooded over, and the wind blew hard against that house. But it did not fall, because it was built on rock. [26] "But anyone who hears these words of mine and does not obey them is like a foolish man who built his house on sand. [27] The rain poured down, the rivers flooded over, the wind blew hard against that house, and it fell. And what a terrible fall that was!

— Matthew 7:24-27 (GNT) —

DAY # 9

Mascot of the Storm

The word "mascot" is defined by Merriam-Webster as a person, animal, or object adopted by a group as a symbolic figure especially to bring them good luck. As Christians, we don't believe in luck—however, we should embrace the positive aspects of a storm. Storms bring out the best and worst in people. Noted motivational speaker and author Joel Osteen once said, *"You can be in the storm, but don't let the storm get in you."* Life in my household can be stormy at times. Being the sole caretaker for my son as well as my mother while juggling a demanding teaching career hasn't always been a picnic. But after the storm, there is a sense of peace and cleansing in the atmosphere.

Storms represent an overcoming spirit through adversity. Please allow me to elaborate...

My 18-year-old son wasn't always as well adjusted as he is today. You see, he was diagnosed with Asperger's Syndrome at age four. He had been kicked out of multiple preschools. This "storm" in my life propelled me to educate myself and tap into resources to help navigate the journey. There were many tearful moments of frustration as well as tears of joyful celebration. By the end of third grade, he was identified as Gifted. New storms arose as I walked a fine line between frustrating him and providing sufficient challenge. There were times when I failed miserably (and he let me know). Being both mom and dad is a daunting task, and I know that many of you can relate. Middle school was a rocky time, to say the least. Some storms are physical and others are purely emotional. When it was time for high school, I could feel the winds of change.

After a rigorous application process, God graciously allowed Corbin to be accepted at McFatter Technical High School. This magnet school was a no-frills place where he could focus like a laser with other students who don't dance to the beat of social expectations. The school environment fit him like a glove, and yet, there were storms during that first year. His grades floundered and he sank before he swam. The mascot of the school is actually a storm and their motto is "Taking the world by Storm." I never realized how appropriate that mascot was on the first day of Corbin's high school career, but when he walked across that stage to graduate with his neck fully decorated in honor cords and accolades, it resonated. He fought through the storm where fierce winds once threatened his future and made it to the other side where a full scholarship awaited him. If storms strengthen us and cleanse the atmosphere, embrace your inner mascot with joy!

Daily Reading

*God quieted the storm to a whisper;
the sea's waves were hushed.*

— PSALMS 107:29 (CEB) —

DAY # 10

Blessing in the Storm

Many South Floridians can relate to the destruction that Hurricane Irma caused back in 2017. My beautiful mobile home sustained structural damage that caused the roof to leak whenever it rained. Unfortunately, home insurance had been cost-prohibitive and I took my chances that year. I went through a season of frustration as I sought repair estimates. I felt depressed and hopeless as my community reminded me that tarps must be temporary (they are supposedly a blight on the community). I applied for FEMA assistance and Small Business loans and became well acquainted with the word "**DENIED**". My mother comes from strong German stock and my father is a Russian Jew whose parents emigrated from their homeland during The Pogroms. Being a quitter is not in my DNA, but I had never been more tempted to throw in the towel in my entire life.

Months later, after many futile appeals, I applied for a brand-new grant initiative with a list of criteria that could choke an elephant! Between working and finding time to comply with every requirement, my time and energy were drained and my emotions were at a breaking point. I wondered where the Lord was through this storm as more complications arose. I would like to say that it was easy and that I knew it would all be fine, but I cried and fell into despair. Nonetheless, I kept moving forward. At times, I crawled through the next hoop with no joy in my heart, only a flicker of hope. People told me that it was a waste of time and that I might never qualify for the program. Sometimes, I agreed. Faith takes necessary action through the storm in spite of personal feelings. The final outcome is that God did above and beyond anything that I could have imagined. We were approved for a brand-new mobile home instead of a repair. Be open to the blessing in the storm and keep God's promises close to your heart. He will NEVER fail you!

Daily Readings

When you pass through the deep, stormy sea, you can count on me to be there with you. When you pass through raging rivers, You will not drown. When you walk through persecution like fiery flames, you will not be burned; the flames will not harm you,

— Isaiah 43:1-2 (TPT) —

Though we experience every kind of pressure, we're not crushed. At times we don't know what to do, but quitting is not an option. We are persecuted by others, but God has not forsaken us. We may be knocked down, but not out.

— 2 Corinthians 4:8-9 (TPT) —

And we know that all things work together for good to those who love God, to those who are the called according to His purpose.

— Romans 8:28 (NKJV)—

DAY # 11

Faith During a Storm

Faith is something like a seed
Faith can spring up out of need
When you need it, that's when it's there.
When others need it, it's something to share
Faith can begin as something small
It seems insignificant and that is all
But as it begins to mature and grow
You learn what you reap is what you sow
So, learn to see with different eyes
Begin to look forward from gray skies
If one spark of hope is all you claim
Then light a match and start the flame

Then you will really begin to know
That faith is with you wherever you go.

I hope that this poem touches your heart and reminds you that faith is not some elusive concept in our lives. It is a gift that often surfaces when you least expect it. God asks us to trust Him as our Good Father who only has our best interests at heart. Diamonds are formed under pressure and it is in those moments of intense adversity that faith grows. Remember to trust the captain of your ship because He knows the route.

Daily Readings

[10] fear not, for I am with you;
be not dismayed, for I am your God;

I will strengthen you, I will help you,
I will uphold you with my righteous right hand.

— Isaiah 41:10 (ESV) —

[20] "Because you're not yet taking God seriously," said
Jesus. "The simple truth is that if you had a mere
kernel of faith, a poppy seed, say, you would tell this
mountain, 'Move!' and it would move. There is
nothing you wouldn't be able to tackle."

— Matthew 17:20 (MSG) —

DAY # 12

Conquering a Storm

This particular anecdote is a shout-out to my son, Corbin. If there is one thing I can say about him, it is that he takes his hobbies seriously. We have run the gamut in this household from an early LEGO obsession to chess matches, basketball, billiards and bowling. He has the heart of a champion and views everything through the lens of competition. He never allowed circumstances (which may have felt like storms through childhood eyes) to dissuade him. For example, when he was rejected by a billiard league because he was 15, he went to the top (behind my back) and was granted an exception.

During his senior year, my son had honed his technique in bowling enough to be competitive. However, his school had no such team! He was given a unique opportunity to join the inaugural team for Western High School. This would prove challenging since he needed approval from his home school to leave early and miss certain days. The next gusts blew when asking my mother to drive him to and from these distant practices. This excited team was big on potential, but short on experience. Many quit, leaving only seven members with the hearts of champions. The first game of the season, these students who had never played together miraculously shot a 217 as a team during the Baker match.

Fast forward to the day of district finals. Corbin was up against the best teams in Broward County and it was discouraging, to say the least. Although it was an honor just to be there, they realized that their day was coming to an end. They were nearing the last game and they took a break to regroup. They rallied each other and said "If we are going to lose, we aren't going down without a fight!" They won their next game and Corbin threw two strikes. Now they had a chance! They had found their rhythm and bowled their way through the storm, annihilating pins and commanding respect that new teams rarely get. They ended the day in a respectable third place position in the district and they were mentioned in The Sun Sentinel local newspaper for their amazing season.

Ironically, all of my son's bowling balls are made by the company, "Storm." He chooses specific balls for different conditions on the lane. One thing that stuck with me was his comment about ball types. "It's the material in the center core that really matters and makes it effective." He said that professionals always have a plan of attack and stick with whatever fails them the least. I challenge you today to remember who you have on the inside. He NEVER fails. Pray. Ask God to give you a strategy to conquer your storm.

Daily Reading

I can do all things through
Christ which strengtheneth me.

— PHILIPPIANS 4:13 (KJV) —

DAY # 13

Storms Bring Balance

Storms have a bad reputation…and for good reason. But have you ever considered that God sometimes uses them to bring about balance in our lives? First, let's take a look at a natural storm's positive impact on the environment. The most obvious effect is that storms often bring about much needed rain. This may benefit crops and provide a reprieve in situations where there has been a problem with drought. Another benefit is that storms offset bacteria and function to break up areas where red tide has accumulated. These unwelcome storms also regulate temperatures globally and provide fresh air to the affected regions. Hurricanes, specifically, replenish inland plant life as well as barrier islands and disperse plant seeds, resulting in more biodiversity. Although harsh winds may blow and topple many older trees, this actually allows the sun to reach areas that were once blocked. Eventually, new canopy trees replace the older ones after this necessary cleansing cycle takes place. Hurricanes may be feared, but perhaps they should be respected and occasionally welcomed like a prescribed fire. God sees the bigger picture and has only our best interests at heart.

Now, as I write this devotional, we are in a situation that none of us could have imagined. A global pandemic and quarantine-I can't think of a more earthshaking storm. Many of us are asking the obvious question. WHY? Even though we are in a dark place right now, I am reminded of the balancing effect of storms. Through all the loss and fear of the moment, I am asking the Lord to show me how to prioritize my life in this season. The busy global schedule has come to a screeching halt, allowing time for reflection.

Here are eight ways that the pandemic has brought more balance into our lives.

1. Quality time with family. (Finding new ways to bond in close quarters.)

2. Tech-free time (decluttering, reading, organizing, board games, writing)

3. Less pollution. We are blessing our planet by traveling less.

4. Creativity. It's amazing how removing distractions can lead to innovation.

5. "We" mentality instead of "Me" mentality. Reminds us to put others first.

6. Motivation to seek God. Let's be honest, we pray more in times of crisis.

7. Financial benefit. Generally speaking, we spend less when stuck at home.

8. Unity. This storm has brought families, churches and communities closer.

Daily Reading

*Ask rain from the Lord in the season of the
spring rain, from the Lord who makes the storm
clouds, and he will give them showers of rain,
to everyone the vegetation in the field.*

— ZECHARIAH 10:1 (ESV) —

DAY # 14

God's Favored in the Storm

Teachers see it a mile away. Parents who go a bit overboard and the child who assumes his position at the center of his parents' universe. Think high maintenance and high expectations. "Only Child Syndrome" is apparently a very recognizable disorder. At least, so it seems. After two unsuccessful pregnancies, and the aftermath of that storm, my miracle child was born. One day in particular strikes me as memorable. I was helping my son, Corbin, to rid his small room of some large clutter. We would donate these "underutilized gems" to Goodwill. He was completely agreeable at first. That was, until I asked him to part with Clifford, The Big Red Dog.

Clifford had become old and tattered (not to mention the fact that he was over three feet tall.) He had not been touched for years and one eye had long ago been surrendered to an army of one—endowed with a permanent marker and a penchant for "all things quirky." I reasoned with my son that Clifford would prefer to be in a home with a child who might truly appreciate him. This finally convinced him and I quickly made my escape to the donation site just before it closed.

The next morning, to my surprise, my son awoke in tears. He could not believe that he had lost his "friend" and he said that he missed his Clifford more than anything. The sobs shook his entire body. Nothing could console him and his anxiety grew with each passing hour. I could feel his despair, so I conceded and went back to the Goodwill site where this dog was surrendered, with cash in hand. After searching the donation trailer, the patient woman explained that the dog was no longer there and may have been shipped to any other Goodwill site in Dade or Broward. I pleaded urgently, "You don't understand. My son **needs** this dog!" She shot me a puzzled look and ventured, "Only child?" I responded, "Yes." With a flash of insight, she gave me a comprehensive list of every Goodwill store in Southeast Florida. She confided, "I too, have only one child and I would probably do the same thing." After many fruitless hours on the phone describing Clifford to hurried store clerks, I resigned myself to a turbulent week of domestic drama. Corbin's red dog vanished from our lives forever. Thankfully, time is a great healer, and laughter soon replaced the tears when we adopted a beautiful rat terrier named Bessie.

This may not sound like much of a storm to you, but through six-year-old eyes, the situation rivals a tidal wave of epic proportions. The love of God is very much like a doting mother's love. He never dismisses our concerns. He loves each of us individually and unconditionally. He has millions of children, and yet He knows each of us by name and has the very hairs on our heads numbered. In fact, He will go to the ends of the earth for you and meet your every unique need. You have a personal relationship with The Captain of your life and that means family privileges! God has reserved a life vest with your name proudly inscribed on it. Yes, He has other children caught in the tempests of life, but you will never find Him too busy to respond to your distress signal and send out the lifeline. The story of the shepherd who leaves the fold of ninety-nine sheep to find the lost one reminds us that every child is equally important to the Lord. Indeed, you live in a family where every child is God's favorite one.

Storms can knock the wind out of your sails and drastically impact your life. People may dismiss your concerns as trivial, and they may even be correct in their assessment. Yet, to the ears of a doting parent, your voice is sweet music and delight. Just think of the goodness of The Lord. He is an involved parent who will never neglect you. I have had friends from large families tell me that sometimes they felt invisible growing up. Yet, in God's sight, every child is unique and validated. Even if you question the purpose of your storm, you will never be disowned. He has chosen you for good reason and He is passionate about His relationship with you. He wants to spoil and shower you with unexpected blessings because you matter that much. He brags about you constantly because you resemble Him! He would have sent Jesus Christ to die for you even if you had been the only one. There is no excuse for you to settle. **You are not an orphan; you are God's favored**, so celebrate His goodness even through this storm!

Daily Readings

As a mother comforts her child, so will I comfort you…

— Isaiah 66:13 (NIV) —

I'm God's favorite.
He made me king of the mountain…

— Psalms 30:7 (MSG) —

The LORD God is like the sun that gives us light. He is like a shield that keeps us safe. The LORD blesses us with favor and honor. He doesn't hold back anything good from those whose lives are without blame.

— Psalm 84:11 (NIRV) —

DAY # 15

The Anchor in the Storm

Fish were meant for the sea and man was meant for dry land. How I wish that I had held to this mantra when a close ministry friend invited me to bring my son for a day of deep-sea fishing and church fellowship. Corbin had recently become obsessed with fishing and his smile was my reward. The day before had been particularly stormy, but our trip was still a go. With fishing poles in hand and hearts full of expectation, we placed our lives in the captain's capable hands and boarded for a day of adventure!

The beginning of the day went smoothly enough as I commented on the incredibly calm waters. This was an

51

unexpected surprise after a rainy night. We joked and chatted easily about how I didn't want to actually kill any of our daily catch and I told my son that it was simply for sport; his disappointment was palpable. Little did I know that we were still in a protected bay area and I was being lulled into a false sense of security. Armed with sunscreen, foul-smelling bait and the knowledge that this was a ministry-related trip, I prayed for a calm and memorable day. Motion sickness had tormented me as a child, but now I bravely ventured closer to the bow for a better view!

Soon enough, we entered the deeper open waters and conditions deteriorated. The anchor went down for what seemed like at least an hour before we were told that the best fishing would be in yet deeper waters. By now, others on board were becoming ill as the waves averaged between five and six feet. Waves of nausea overcame our group with no end in sight. The anchor went down into the deepest area and we never moved far because the anchor kept us hopelessly grounded for the long haul, in spite of relentless waves. Excited veteran fisherman greeted us with shouts to announce that our fishing poles were bending under the weight of hungry fish that we had no desire to conquer (while lying on couches in the hull of the boat next to a ready receptacle).

Prayers of "Peace, Be Still" did not work and neither did my shameless pitch to pay the captain to bring us back ashore. After all, the seasoned fishermen were having the time of their lives anchored in paradise with fish practically jumping aboard. This day was definitely one for the books—or at least one to include in this devotional. The take-away is that storms WILL come but Christ is our anchor. His Word is a constant that keeps us from drifting. The boat of life may rock, but **HE is your stabilizing force.**

Daily Reading

*We have this hope as an anchor for the soul, firm and
secure. It enters the inner sanctuary behind the curtain.*

— HEBREWS 6:19 (NIV) —

DAY # 16

The Ark in the Storm

The Biblical account of Noah building the ark has become one of the most recognizable stories in the Old Testament. The mandate to build the ark was not popular; in fact, Noah was quite the outcast when he acted on the word of The Lord and built an ark, defying all common sense. The God of the Old Testament was known for judgment, but He rewarded faithfulness and righteousness. In Genesis 7:1, we see the dynamics: "And the Lord said unto Noah, Come thou and all thy house into the ark; for thee have I seen righteous before me in this generation." (KJV) God was calling Noah and his family to a higher place without giving all the details.

He promised His protection, yet demanded a commitment that was inconvenient and irrational. In essence, He required Noah's entire family to submit to a time of quarantine; this was not going to be a picnic.

The ark was a place of refuge and solitude. The storms and rain eventually pounded the ark, but their safety was assured. Traditional wisdom recommends safety in numbers, yet God sometimes allows isolation for protection. God established lines of demarcation between His People (The Israelites) and the Egyptians. There were separate rules of decorum, worship, food preparation and daily conduct. The protection of the Lord was always contingent upon obedience. The earth was just as morally bankrupt then as it is now, but the ark was a place of provision in the middle of global chaos. A good parent would never watch a disaster unfold without sounding the alarm. God speaks to us in the stillness. Disasters and pandemics are nothing new; we live in an imperfect world.

When God protects His children through stormy conditions, He is very particular about the rules of engagement. The ark was constructed of wood and there was only one access door. The ark was sealed according to God's specifications and any discrepancy may have resulted in disaster. During this season of pandemic, being constrained and quarantined may seem like a burden, and yet I challenge you to consider the ark. Think of your home and the people you love as "the called-out ones" and embrace this moment. Don't fight against the advice to shelter in place. Consider it a blessing to be at home.

Daily Readings

Come, my people, enter your chambers, and shut your doors behind you; hide yourselves for a little while until the fury has passed by.

— Isaiah 26:20 (ESV) —

Therefore, come out from among unbelievers, and separate yourselves from them, says the LORD. Don't touch their filthy things, and I will welcome you.

— II Corinthians 6:17 (NLT) —

DAY # 17

The Rainbow After the Storm

Rainbows are an eternal symbol of divine promise, hope and love. I reference this sign based on a clear Biblical distinction alone (not any movement or agenda). Rainbows glisten with the fire and light of an ancient promise that still resonates today! It amazes me that God's perfect love is the most visible in our lives **after** we have endured a storm.

Song: "Love Me Like a Rainbow"

Verse
You add color to my world because You are the light
A promise spoken softly in the middle of my night
You have no beginning, and the end I'll never find
In the middle of the chaos, You bring comfort to my mind

Chorus (Repeat until the end)
Father, love me like a rainbow
spreading high above the storm
I will follow where You lead me
And Your love is my reward-
Your reflection is my purpose
Every word You speak is true
I reach out in faith to touch You
Like a rainbow-I love You!

Daily Readings

I have set my rainbow in the clouds, and it will be the sign of the covenant between me and the earth.

— GENESIS 9:13 (NIV) —

And the one who sat there had the appearance of jasper and ruby. A rainbow that shone like an emerald encircled the throne.

— REVELATION 4:3 (NIV) —

DAY # 18

Ode to the Storm

Rocking. Reeling. Drowsily awake.
I surrender to this storm. For greater things.
You call to me and bid me to open the door wide
As the wind whips through my heart and mind

"Why?" I ask. And then, I quiet myself
Uncharted waters. Ominous, yet purposeful.
The seawall overtaken; even so Your habitation
A plethora of questions, defy explanation

Can dead bones live after the storm?
Do seeds grow in spite of parched soil?
Pain makes no pretense of allure-
But Oh, the work it does when I mature!

Crimson rain drives the whitest snow
A residue of purest gold
Sacrifice a corpse of evergreen, now dull
To produce transfiguration.

Daily Reading

Dear friends, don't be surprised about the fiery
trials that have come among you to test you.
These are not strange happenings.

— I Peter 4:12 (CEB) —

DAY # 19

Asleep in the Storm

Storms evoke powerful emotions. In fact, most of us do our best to avoid them. We check the weather and make plans that circumvent the very possibility of rain. Our comfort zone is dry, predictable and sunny (perhaps with an occasional shower to water a newly planted garden). Life is good when it happens on our terms and no one prays for stormy conditions. Personally, my happy place is silent. But I have a close friend who clings to her sound machine (with rain, thunder and breezy conditions) as "white noise" to help her sleep. Experts believe that rain soothes the senses and tempts us to hit the snooze button. Yet, being stuck outside under these conditions would be quite traumatic. Red danger flags begin waving as soon as the skies darken; sane people take cover ahead of the storm. Survival gurus rarely mention sleep as a viable tactic for managing a crisis.

As a believer in Christ, I have often wondered about how Jesus could sleep in the middle of a storm. Didn't He know that the storm was coming before setting sail? The storm's intensity was no exaggeration since the most seasoned fishermen on the vessel feared for their lives. Yes, they had seen the many miracles that Jesus performed, and yet, in that moment, anxiety had a much louder voice than faith. Considering my weak stomach when marine conditions are not optimal, it baffles me that anyone could block out a raging storm. The confidence in this very act borders on smug indifference. God manifested in humanity was utterly exhausted from ministry. Why stress over such a minor issue when He knew the end of the story? To Christ, a storm was soothing white noise. Insomnia, depression and anxiety are the scourge of modern life. Don't surrender your peace. You have inside information on the crisis. Hit the snooze button. You win!

Daily Readings

²³ Then he got into the boat and his disciples followed him. ²⁴ Suddenly a furious storm came up on the lake, so that the waves swept over the boat. But Jesus was sleeping. ²⁵ The disciples went and woke him, saying, "Lord, save us! We're going to drown!"

²⁶ He replied, "You of little faith, why are you so afraid?" Then he got up and rebuked the winds and the waves, and it was completely calm.

²⁷ The men were amazed and asked, "What kind of man is this? Even the winds and the waves obey him!"

— Matthew 8:23-27 (NIV) —

This is My command: be strong and courageous. Never be afraid or discouraged because I am your God, the Eternal One, and I will remain with you wherever you go.

—Joshua 1:9 (VOICE) —

DAY # 20

Emotional Storms

Storms can wreak havoc on communities and businesses. In fact, history books are replete with details of unexpected storm fallout. Political campaigns have crumbled when a politician appeared "too distant" following a major disaster. To be sure, the human, emotional and financial toll of storms can be devastating. In general, local residents become familiar enough with local weather patterns to calculate their risk. Advances in meteorology have made storm forecasting more accurate than ever before. Yet, for all of the innovative technology that exists, there has been no breakthrough; these monsters tear through luxurious cities and remote villages indiscriminately. Some argue that global warming plays a major role in the development of storms. Regardless of the cause, the effects of a natural storm can be painful to experience.

In much the same way, emotional pain wreaks havoc on our lives. In essence, the unseen hurts and wounds that we carry are an internal storm. Many of us try to cope with anxiety, depression, insecurity and guilt while daily masquerading into numb oblivion. Sometimes, volunteering or ministering to others may even prove to be a worthy distraction. Yet the truth remains that many of us have unresolved emotional storms in our lives. This world is imperfect and broken. Some of us have been hurt by our parents, partners or friends. Maybe life handed you a situation that was unfair and the deck was stacked against you through no fault of your own. The book of Psalms is full of emotional storms and David cried out to The Lord in moments of deep anguish. Emotional pain does not point to a lack of faith. It points to humanity.

Christianity has done a disservice to many people by shaming their emotional pain and causing them to "stuff their emotions" while confessing the victory. Jesus himself had moments (in his humanity) where he felt sadness, loneliness, frustration and anger. We should confront the emotional storms in our lives and ask God to show us how to navigate. That may require forgiveness or an uncomfortable conversation that we dread. Being a

Christian is not an immediate fix-all for dysfunction. You may have been abused or rejected by the one you trusted the most. I would be lying to say that dark moments in your life are always short-lived seasons. Protracted emotional storms are the ones that lead to feelings of isolation and hopelessness. I have been there and the truth is that even the most loyal friends can grow weary of chronic venting. It's ok to be authentic and transparent with God. He is fully invested and will never leave. This cruel storm will spend itself and you will smile again, full of contagious hope.

Daily Reading

He healeth the broken in heart,
and bindeth up their wounds.

— Psalm 147:3 (KJV) —

DAY # 21

Spiritual Storms

A beacon. Hope. A promise made.
I know You walk with me.
Yet struggles sometimes seem to last for an eternity.
Clouds have blocked my clarity and I can't see Your face.
Blindly, still I stumble onward continuing the race.
Feelings. Unreliable. Yet, unrelenting.
Am I alone in this place? Lord, I need an infusion of grace.
The tumult of doubt and fear is suffocating.
And sometimes, the hardest part of faith is waiting.
Redemptive. Cleansing. Changing.
These are storms from God's own hand.
Confusing. Tempting. Destroying.

Crafted in darkness by Satan's plan.

Lord, You have a purpose. You have a reason.

The victory is promised even through this season.

So, I ask for discernment. The plan of attack.

When to move forward and when to step back.

Your beacon shines and darkness hides.

The tempest will subside.

Strengthen my resolve and spirit. Lord, please be my guide.

Daily Readings

For we wrestle not against flesh and blood, but against principalities, against powers, against the rulers of the darkness of this world, against spiritual wickedness in high places.

— Ephesians 6:12 (KJV) —

Keep a cool head. Stay alert.
The Devil is poised to pounce, and would like nothing better than to catch you napping.

— 1 Peter 5:8 (MSG) —

DAY # 22

Storms of Sickness

When sickness threatened the life of a dear friend of mine named Octavio, it was not just a blustery day; this was tsunami territory. For a few months, his health had been declining. A notable lack of energy and overall malaise sent warning signals that something was very wrong. He began to cry out to God for healing only to hear these words in his spirit, "You are sick, but I'm going to heal you." Days later, he awoke to find that his urine was the color of Coca-Cola. Reluctantly, he went to the doctor to receive the shocking news that he had hepatitis C. The viral load and drastically elevated liver enzymes signaled that his liver was already in shutdown mode. How could this happen? He was a man of faith, a devoted husband and father. Day and night, he cried out to the living God from the depths of his soul. Again, he heard the voice of God (in a way that few people ever experience) give him clear instructions about his next steps. I vividly remember the day in 2013, sitting by the lake in my community, when I received the enthusiastic call. Octavio said that he knew he was supposed to go see a specific evangelist named Ted Shuttlesworth, and that God would use this person to manifest his healing! I wanted to believe, yet my rational mind wondered if this was faith or presumption. Things went from bad to worse, and he spent five days in the hospital and received the dire verdict of acute liver necrosis (death). Specialists warned that his only hope was to be transported to the University of Miami and placed on a waiting list to receive a liver transplant.

Octavio set his mind and heart to follow God's leading and decided to obey divine protocol instead of professional wisdom. He called his wife and insisted that she pick him up from the hospital. By this point, he was twenty pounds lighter and suffered from constant nausea, dehydration, jaundice and persistent itchy and bleeding skin. There was no quality of life for either of them anymore. They carefully checked the evangelist's itinerary and realized that there were no local revivals scheduled. However, the following week, Reverend Shuttlesworth was to hold an outdoor tent meeting in Roxboro, North Carolina. Octavio's shocking decision turned a few heads; he would purchase a one-way ticket, because there was no way to predict the outcome. "Either I die or God heals me" was his stoic approach to this storm. Ultimately, he decided to make the journey alone. There are times when you know that a situation is beyond human intervention and you desperately need precious solitude with God. He gingerly boarded the plane (struggling with his luggage in a physically weakened state) and landed at his destination. When he rented a car and found his hotel, a continual mental battle waged. The ominous view of the county morgue greeted him just outside of his hotel window! Fear and unbelief attempted to steal his promise and dreams of death haunted him saying "You're next."

The first night of the revival was enough to discourage even the most ardent seeker. Rev. Ted Shuttlesworth was not in attendance due to his own father's death. Unflinching, Octavio stayed the course and fought through the disappointment; he would not be denied. He didn't know what to expect the second night, but he had a word from The Lord and trusted that God would honor this act of blind faith. Shuttlesworth returned to conduct the rest of the meetings that week in spite of his own personal grief. **On June 25, 2013,** the service was ending when Shuttlesworth suddenly turned around, stopped and walked directly back to where Octavio was sitting. With deliberate focus, he moved in and spoke with authority: "You know why you're here. Don't you? You have been given a death sentence and God is here to heal you." At that moment, he declared that my afflicted friend would be made whole and he laid his hands on him in faith. To be sure, this minister had no idea that Octavio had followed a specific word from God nor sacrificed so much to attend. The nausea immediately left him and he began to feel strength enter his body. I will never forget the call I received at one o'clock in the morning from his wife, Trudy (my lifelong friend). She was crying and I assumed the worst from her faltering voice. I felt my anxiety building when I posed the obvious question. "What happened?" Through her tears she managed, "It's Octavio…" Thoughts of dread bombarded my (now fully awake) mind. *How will she ever pick up the pieces? What can I say to comfort her now? God, please help me not to say anything stupid.* "Wendy, are you listening? Octavio is healed!" she shouted.

Faith requires action. That same night, Octavio went to the local Walmart and bought a large box of fried chicken. Until that point, he was fortunate to be able to keep down even a small piece of fruit. His appetite returned and he excitedly asked locals to take his picture eating chicken! I can only imagine the amused reactions in that small town, but that didn't matter to him. Energized, he ambled through the city, grinning as he passed the morgue. Upon returning home, the rest of Octavio's healing was more gradual. Eventually, the white color returned to his eyes and the weight returned to his body. His medical records confirm no trace of hepatitis C and completely normal liver enzymes. I do not believe that he would be healed today if he had ignored God's prompting. When a storm of sickness arises, it does not mean that you have done something wrong. On the contrary, this may be a test of your faith. God does not want to be your Plan B. He insists on being your everything! I share this true story to remind you that nothing is impossible. Storms of sickness exist because we live in an imperfect world. When you see the waves approach, cling to faith in the solid rock of God's love because healing is your birthright.

Daily Reading

19 *"LORD, help!" they cried in their trouble,
and he saved them from their distress.*

20 *He sent out his word and healed them,
snatching them from the door of death.*

— Psalm 107:19-20 (NLT) —

DAY # 23

Family Storms

Have you ever listened to someone tell the tale of their once-in-a-lifetime family vacation or read a Facebook post about a "perfect" weekend of marital bliss and felt just a pang of jealousy creep into your heart? Maybe your family situation is less than ideal or perhaps there are some dysfunctional people in your clan that make you shrink back in horror when it is your turn to host for the holidays. People always share their best day-NOT the worst one- and the truth is that you don't know what goes on behind closed doors in those "perfect" family homes with the white picket fence and brand-new cars in the driveway. Family dynamics are complicated by the stressful pace of modern life and unrealistic expectations and compounded by social media as well as the entertainment industry. Let's face it. We often give our best to strangers and save the leftovers for our family because we are usually drained by the time we open the front door.

Family storms can be brutal territory. The people who know us best can always push our buttons better than anyone else. A vast array of emotions like guilt, fear, anger, insecurity and disappointment may cause permanent damage within the family unit. Christians are not immune to the challenging conditions that threaten their happy homes. The only policy available to cover your family and guard against storms is God's Word. It is imperative to stay connected with your representative. Jesus Christ is the mediator between God and man and He is touched by everything that impacts us. The biggest threats to household unity are broken trust and selfishness. Regardless of the specific situation, prayer is the place to start the healing process. If you can gather in prayer, that is ideal, yet if that is not feasible, find someone else that you trust to agree with you. Ask the Lord to repair the damaged hearts and choose to work on yourself.

Family storms are not predictable, but there are usually a few warning signs that someone in the family may need more attention. Be sensitive to **conditions that are**

unusually stressful because they can make your household more vulnerable to storms. Here are just a few:

1. **Disconnection** (lack of communication and everyone going in opposite directions)

2. **Unexpected Major Illness** (shock, grief, loss of independence, financial impacts)

3. **Bad Decisions** (immoral, selfish or foolish choices that impact the family bond)

4. **Depression or Mental Health Disorders** (may trigger verbal or emotional abuse)

5. **Financial Hardship** (loss of steady job or a new weighty financial responsibility)

Daily Readings

*It is truly wonderful when relatives
live together in peace.*

— PSALMS 133:1 (CEV) —

*And over all these virtues put on love,
which binds them all together in perfect unity.*

— COLOSSIANS 3:14 (NIV) —

DAY # 24

Financial Storms

Financial storms are the enemy of progress. They speak failure over our lives and threaten our futures. These storms don't usually brew overnight and hit unexpectedly like a tornado. They are much subtler than that. In fact, they are more of a gradual downward slope leading to a pool of despair. But, there is a way out. Many financial storms happen because of unexpected changes in circumstance. Perhaps a major source of income was lost or an unforeseen medical expense is choking your entire household budget. God sees the frustration that you feel and He is touched by the situation. He is The Father who cares and wants you to rely on Him as your provider.

While God stands ready to intervene, He also requires us to use wisdom in the areas that are controllable, such as discretionary spending. I learned that lesson the hard way and went through many years of credit card debt agony. In my case, I used shopping to numb some personal pain that I didn't want to face. It was an easy (and morally acceptable) escape. There were other times in my life when the struggle was not self-imposed. Sometimes, the only car that you can afford to purchase is the one with the highest risk of expensive future repairs. Check. Been there. If you are the family breadwinner, there is no more helpless feeling than treading water (gasping for air) and juggling bills just to avoid sinking deeper into debt.

On a practical level, seek advice from people with a gift for financial stewardship and consider joining a small group at church for some accountability. I am not an expert yet, but I am on the weaker side of the financial storm and I am not the person I used to be. Let's say, I am still a work in progress. Every situation requires a different strategy, but the important thing is to seek God for the solution that works for you. I was able to settle most of my debts and learn some money-saving techniques that blessed my family. Hard work is non-negotiable; financial adversity won't be conquered without sweat and determination. There were periods of working long hours (seven days a week) just to catch up. Sometimes you need to advocate for your family or negotiate better terms on a credit card or auto insurance. Diligence and consistency will pay off in big dividends, but change begins with you; cycles of financial hardship have to be disrupted by a change in mindset. **Prosperity is possible. God is your source. You were born for success. Your present position does not dictate the outcome of your life.** Make good choices today and tomorrow. Safeguard your finances through Biblical principles and wait out the storm. There may be a creative solution that you didn't consider. Tune out the howling financial winds and tune in to the gentle voice of your Creator. His financial services are free!

Daily Reading

And my God will liberally supply (fill until full)
your every need according to His riches
in glory in Christ Jesus.

— PHILIPPIANS 4:19 (AMP) —

DAY # 25

Church Storms

I grew up never having to scramble to make weekend plans or choose which movie to see with a friend. My mother was taking me to church and the movie was a non-starter. Needless to say, I was raised under strict standards where church attendance was as normal as breathing. But as I grew older, I realized that church is not an obligation or a set of imposed rules-it is a chance to grow and connect with a spiritual family and experience the grace of God. Church can provide an oasis of refreshment that gives us strength to face challenges in our everyday lives. So, what happens when a church family experiences a storm? First, we must check in with ourselves to make sure that we are not contributing to the problem. Unrealistic expectations often lead to disappointment with the leadership or the vision of the church. It can be tempting to engage in gossip or to become critical of the ministry. Church dynamics are very similar to marriages that have a "honeymoon period" where everything seems perfect. But true commitment requires us to demonstrate grace to those who need it most and deserve it least. This can heal a congregation.

I have witnessed my share of church drama, and it is never a pretty sight. Storms attack churches even more violently, at times, than our personal lives. This happens because the devil knows we are stronger united than we are divided. **There are times when there is a valid reason to seek another church (shelter) during a storm, but it should be a last resort.** For instance,

- The leadership is no longer seeking the heart of God. Church has become a business.

- The church has become a place of compromise with excuses for moral failure of leaders.

- There is a heavy spirit of control, abuse or pride with no regard for the people.

- The teaching has dangerously shifted in a direction that is against the Word of God.

Outside of these situations, loyalty goes a long way during church storms and it is beautiful when a church weathers a storm in unity. This pleases the heart of God. I have made the mistake of jumping ship prematurely a couple of times because I was hurt and confrontation makes me feel uncomfortable. The Lord needs all hands on deck more than ever before. It's time to grow thicker skin and stay the course. Families stick together and build a lasting legacy. If there is one thing that the COVID-19 pandemic has exposed, it is individual vulnerability. We are fighting a new breed of storm and the paradigm of "church" was forced to shift drastically online to meet the spiritual needs of an isolated community. So, the church sailed against the wind and rose to the challenge, embracing new technology and reaching the broken. What an extraordinary ship!

Daily Reading

The whole body depends on Christ, and all the parts of the body are joined and held together. Each part does its own work to make the whole body grow and be strong with love.

— Ephesians 4:16 (NCV) —

DAY # 26

Career Storms

For many people, the word "career" is synonymous with "personal identity." At no other time since The Great Depression have so many people been without that sense of security. As I write this devotional during a virtual national lockdown, jobless claims are at an all time high. Restaurants are floundering to remain in business with only take-out and delivery options provided. Pastors and worship leaders have lost their live congregation and moved to a virtual audience, completely reinventing their duties based on changing expectations. For those with careers in the beauty industry, there is no Plan B. They must close their doors and make some tough decisions in the middle of this storm. The travel industry has come to a violent halt (almost overnight) and the audacious doctors, nurses, first responders and essential employees who were able to keep their jobs now risk their lives carrying out their duties each day. Some willingly calculated the cost when they submitted that resume; for others, the perils became incumbent. The harsh winds of change are blowing through every industry and redefining our priorities.

How should we respond to a career storm when everything within us wants to give up? Maybe this hits home and you are one of the many people wondering what comes next. Perhaps you were forced into a job change that you didn't anticipate. When you come to a fork in the road, it is important to realize that this decision is not your own. **God created you for a purpose and He designed you for maximum impact in this world.** Slow down. Breathe. You may feel a tremendous amount of anxiety about your next move, but consider how expert chess players quietly strategize before taking any action. If your back is against the wall and there is no financial cushion, pray for direction and consider a short-term solution (such as temp work) until you have clarity from God. Whether you face a detour or a complete road block, The Lord will never allow your struggle to be wasted. There is a lesson to be learned and a destiny to be embraced. The biggest enemy of destiny is fear, so don't dismiss ideas that intimidate you. Finally, remember that titles are a man-made construct; **only the finished work of Christ defines you.** The ministry of Jesus began after much of His life had been spent in the carpentry trade. Likewise, there are several accounts in The Gospels of disciples who made bold career changes. The winds of change are turning titles into confetti, but **your God-given purpose is secure!**

Daily Readings

For I know the plans I have for you," declares the LORD, "plans to prosper you and not to harm you, plans to give you hope and a future.

— Jeremiah 29:11 (NIV) —

The LORD says, "I will teach you the way you should go; I will instruct you and advise you.

— Psalm 32:8 (GNT)—

DAY # 27

Storms of Rejection

Acceptance. The word has a beautiful ring to it and the warmth literally radiates through my body when I say it out loud. In fact, many of us have spent years of our lives searching in vain for human acceptance. Children are especially vulnerable; parental rejection has a sting that can last for many years. Unfortunately, cycles of rejection tend to repeat themselves from one generation to the next, so that awkward critical comment may have honestly been intended to motivate you! Generally speaking, people walk in the light that they have and they interact with others based on their own experience. I have to remind myself of this fact quite often. Personally, my mind races at warp speed (which sometimes warps my thinking and opens the door for assumptions). God created every human being with a sense of belonging. Sometimes in my own life, I have overcommitted myself or placed my happiness on lay-a-way (this from a shopaholic) thinking that being a people-pleaser would lead to acceptance. (Spoiler alert: Not happening.) Most of us will avoid "rocking the boat" just to steer clear of rejection. Let's face it. Whether rejection comes from your family, spouse, friend or a trusted colleague, the hurt is palpable. The forceful winds of rejection destroy our self-esteem and feel like a sucker-punch to the heart.

Can we prepare for storms of rejection? Not always. To do so would be to fortify our hearts and make them impenetrable. God gave us emotions for a reason and He wants us to love those around us with abandon. However, that does not mean that we should surround ourselves with people who trigger pain. I am learning that boundaries are a good thing and they can protect us from moving off course. If you have made your feelings known to someone who disregards your hurt and intentionally (repeatedly) inflicts emotional pain, then you may have to devise an emergency procedure to prevent casualties. As with any storm, trust your instruments to safely navigate to the other side. The Holy Spirit is our Comfortor and Guide through the billowing sea of rejection. **You are not a castaway.** It might help to remember that people are not always aware that their words or body language may trigger intense feelings of hurt. Jesus is always aware and He can relate to feelings of rejection better than anyone. You are accepted by Him and there are no conditions on that love because it is perfect. Choose to accept yourself today. No excuses!

Daily Readings

⁹⁻¹⁰ You've always been right there for me; don't turn your back on me now. Don't throw me out, don't abandon me; you've always kept the door open. My father and mother walked out and left me, but God took me in.

— Psalm 27:9-10 (MSG) —

As you come to him, a living stone rejected by men but in the sight of God chosen and precious,

— 1 Peter 2:4 (ESV)—

DAY # 28

Firestorms

Residents of sunny California know it all too well. The word, "firestorm" is defined by Merriam-Webster as a very intense and destructive fire usually accompanied by high winds. Many of these fires are triggered by the actions of human beings. Firestorms also refer to debates and arguments that take on monstrous proportions and threaten one's future. Indeed, a "firestorm" of intense criticism can bring the best of us to our knees. Arguments and character assassination are nothing new. In the Bible, Joseph was a good man, and yet God allowed firestorms to build his character and pave the way for destiny (but not before he spent time in prison due to false accusations). A firestorm is fueled by surrounding air which allows the strongest winds to surround the fire and move inward. Firestorms are incredibly intense and unpredictable, usually creating the most severe damage when the area is tinder dry. Tornado force winds are a common feature. These firestorms literally create their own energy and will not subside until they have consumed everything in their path. Gossip and strife are no different; they create their own negative energy and reduce reputations to ashes. A firestorm is not pretty.

As believers, how should we respond to an unexpected firestorm? First, nothing can be resolved without prayer. If we respond to others from a place of sheer emotion, the outside winds of strife will intensify the problem and eventually consume us. Have you ever tried to defend yourself in an argument only to realize that you didn't filter your words but instead escalated the situation and fueled the dispute? I certainly have! Remember that The Bible is water to our souls and we are less vulnerable to firestorms when we are fully soaked in God's Word and presence. Don't attempt to deal with a firestorm unless you are first drenched with fresh insight after a time of devotion. Arguments are inevitable, because we are human. However, disagreements worsen if we allow our negative thoughts (and even well-meaning people) to provoke us further. Keep a cool head. Remember that a firestorm consumes anything that is dry and combustible, so ask God to give you a pure heart that can be tried by fire and come through as gold. When we respond to firestorms with the right attitude, we de-escalate the situation and view others through a different lens. Harmony will replace this confusing season of discord. You can walk through a firestorm and emerge without even the smell of smoke on your clothing. Jesus walks with you!

Daily Readings

"Look!" he answered, "I see four men loose, walking in the midst of the fire; and they are not hurt, and the form of the fourth is like the Son of God."

— Daniel 3:25 (NKJV) —

Where there is no fuel a fire goes out; where there is no gossip arguments come to an end.

— Proverbs 26:20 (CEV) —

DAY # 29

Dancing Through the Storm

I pray that the song, "Dancing Through the Storm" reawakens your childlike hope and wonder. Reframe the ominous concept of your storm as an adventure and allow Christ to lead the way!

1. Focus on your partner as He turns your life around
   Holding hands and spinning with
   His voice the only sound
   Full of wonder like a child, just take a leap of faith.
   Frolic through the raging tide.
   It's time to take your place.

Chorus
The waves are just a dancefloor.
You are dancing in the deep.
He holds you up. You will not fall.
This is the last dance. Give it your all!

2. So, dance with abandon.
   'Cause joy comes in the morning.
   Your moves are one in a million.
   You're non-conforming.
   Beautiful tempest. Hurricane of the strongest love.
   Carries you towards destiny to music from above.

Refrain
Dancing Through the Storm (4x)

Daily Readings

Once again I will rebuild you.
Once again you will take up your tambourines
and dance joyfully.

— JEREMIAH 31:4 (GNT) —

Trust God from the bottom of your heart;
don't try to figure out everything on your own.

— PROVERBS 3:5 (MSG) —

DAY # 30

Clear Skies and a Heartbeat

There is nothing quite like the feeling of waking up to a clear sky, knowing that the worst is over and the best is yet to come. For many animals, hibernation is the best way to cope with the worst of the winter storms. It is a season of dormancy and inactivity for many animals as well as seasonal plants. I was never much of a science whiz, but the topic of hibernation fascinated me on many levels. How could animals slow down their breathing and heart rates and go months without any food consumption? (New diet fad, perhaps?) This survival tactic actually helps them to conserve energy during stormy winter months. Frogs (certainly not my favorite) know how to cheat death! In the article, "*Playing Dead For The Next Hundred Years*" Justin Nobel explains, "As the cold comes, wood frogs burrow inside logs or beneath rocks or leaf piles. Their hearts stop, they stop breathing and ice crystals form in their blood, which actually helps keep their cells warmer. Roughly two-thirds of their body water is completely frozen." This means that something within protects them from dying when all the odds are stacked against them. Our protection during every storm comes from within, because The Greater One lives inside of us.

For many, being on lockdown during a pandemic feels like hibernation; we all wonder when this season will end. Perhaps you are grieving the loss of our collective freedom to attend church services or social gatherings. Or, maybe there is a much more deeply personal loss that you and God alone understand. Whatever storm you have been facing, the good news is that trials have an expiration date. The skies will clear and the warm sun will shine on your face again. There is a song that encouraged me during a very dark season in my life. It was Danny Gokey's "Tell Your Heart To Beat Again." Sometimes we need reassurance that our hearts will eventually heal from pain. During winter storms in our lives, we need to conserve our energy and rest in Our Creator. This past weekend, Good Friday felt very different. Most of us reflected on The Crucifixion privately in our homes and the eerie significance was palpable. The world has never been in a stormier season. That Friday afternoon, Christ's death impacted nature; darkness fell and an earthquake shook the land. But at that moment, God incarnate conquered every storm that you and I would ever face. **On Sunday, there were clear skies and a heartbeat.** He is alive!

Daily Readings

⁵ The angel said to the women, "Don't be afraid! I know you are looking for Jesus, who was nailed to a cross. ⁶ He isn't here! God has raised him to life, just as Jesus said he would. Come, see the place where his body was lying.

— Matthew 28:5-6 (CEV) —

In peace I will lie down and sleep.
LORD, you alone keep me safe.

— Psalm 4:8 (NIRV) —

Storm Chasers
Study Guide & Tips

For our light and momentary troubles
are achieving for us an eternal glory
that far outweighs them all.

— 2 CORINTHIANS 4:17 (NIV) —

The content in the following pages will encourage you to interact with the themes of each devotional. The storm survey questions will foster deeper reflection either individually or in a group setting. The question sets correspond to each day of your devotional journey. I encourage you to respond to each question because it will help you to personally connect with the text. If you are in a group study, the leader may facilitate a time to share these responses. (This should be completely optional and non-judgmental) Be flexible and sensitive during this exercise.

You will find some helpful storm statements after the questions. These statements are affirmations of faith that will strengthen your resolve to be a storm chaser instead of a storm evader. Finally, there is a prayer of salvation at the very end. Jesus is calling you to walk on water, but you must take the first step and accept Him as your Savior. If you are already a believer, this guide may be a helpful icebreaker for sharing Christ with someone today. The lockdown is a shared experience that has triggered global anxiety. In the eye of this storm, there is stillness and hope for today.

Storm Survey
Day 1

- How much do I trust God for protection?

- What does God's will look like in my life?

- What patterns cause fear to surface in my life?

- When do I usually feel the closest to God?

- What can I do differently in my next storm?

What is God speaking to my heart?

Storm Survey
Day 2

- What am I most grateful for right now?

- How do I usually express thankfulness?

- How did my priorities shift during the pandemic?

- Why should I be thankful during trials?

- How do I define the word "surrender?"

What is God speaking to my heart?

Storm Survey
Day 3

- What promises has God made to me?

- What is my purpose here on earth?

- Why does the word "obey" evoke such a negative reaction in me or others? Examine this.

- How am I making a difference in lives right now?

- What excuses block me from reaching my destiny?

What is God speaking to my heart?

Storm Survey Day 4

- Do I have realistic expectations of others during trials?

- How do I approach God when I need comfort?

- Can I reflect back on a time when God intervened in my life and use my story to inspire someone?

- Do I usually approach prayer as a first or last resort during challenging seasons in my life?

- Which words come to mind first when I hear the name, *Jesus?*

What is God speaking to my heart?

Storm Survey
Day 5

- How does God demonstrate His kindness?

- What is the difference between a *calling* and an *obligation*?

- How do I represent God in my sphere of influence?

- Am I willing to step out of my comfort zone?

- What is God's assignment for me today?

What is God speaking to my heart?

Storm Survey
Day 6

- What dreams have I placed on hold?

- How can I spiritually prepare for a storm?

- How has social distancing impacted me?

- What personal issues can I confront now?

- How do I feel about the unknown?

What is God speaking to my heart?

Storm Survey
Day 7

- What song ministers to me during a storm?

- Am I a storm *chaser* or a storm *evader*?

- How can I hear God's quiet voice during a storm?

- How can I apply James 1: 2-4 to my life now?

- What is the best way for me to overcome fear?

What is God speaking to my heart?

Storm Survey
Day 8

- How can I strengthen my *storm dwelling*?

- Is my life a habitation for God's presence?

- What do I consider to be *minor damage*?

- What are some things that might make my spirit *inaccessible*?

- What usually helps me to reset after my life is disrupted by a storm?

What is God speaking to my heart?

Storm Survey
Day 9

- Why do storms represent an overcoming spirit?

- How are my moods impacted by trials?

- Do I surrender to change or resist it?

- Is there a challenge that I have been afraid to accept?

- Can I remember a specific storm that fostered growth in my life?

What is God speaking to my heart?

Storm Survey
Day 10

- Do I believe that God is disappointed in me?

- Why might God disguise a blessing within a storm?

- Can faith and fear coexist? Please explore this.

- There is an old adage: "God helps those who help themselves." Do I agree or disagree? Explain.

- When was the last time that God showed up during a storm in my life? Did I recognize His presence? Why or why not?

What is God speaking to my heart?

Storm Survey
Day 11

- How does pressure add value to my life?

- Why does the Bible compare faith to a seed?

- Have I taken advantage of opportunities to share my faith or encourage someone who was weak?

- What characteristics qualify God as a *Good Father*?

- What does it look like to walk in faith during seasons of adversity?

What is God speaking to my heart?

Storm Survey Day 12

- What does it mean to have the heart of a champion?

- How do I respond when faced with a challenge?

- Can I remember a situation in which I beat the odds and surprised myself?

- How did others respond to my success?

- What self-defeating attitudes have I adopted and how can I embrace a can-do mentality instead?

What is God speaking to my heart?

Storm Survey
Day 13

- How can storms balance my life?

- Why does God choose fire to refine us?

- Did the lockdown come with any benefits?

- What am I learning through my storm?

- How do my priorities differ from God's and how can I align them?

What is God speaking to my heart?

Storm Survey
Day 14

- Do I realize the extent of God's love for me?

- Have my perceptions of God been shaped by my own family experiences?

- Is God's love ever conditional? Why or why not?

- What connotations come to mind when I hear the words "only child?"

- What does it look like to be *God's favored*?

What is God speaking to my heart?

Storm Survey
Day 15

- How is hope an *anchor* for my soul?

- Do I trust God in the open waters of my life?

- What is my personal comfort zone?

- What kinds of distractions cause me to drift off course and is there a way to prevent them?

- Has God placed a mentor in my life to help steer me through stormy waters? If not, am I taking full advantage of spiritual resources?

What is God speaking to my heart?

Storm Survey Day 16

- What does the ark symbolize to me?

- Noah was shunned for his blind obedience. Do I ever feel like an outcast?

- Under what conditions might God require a period of isolation? Why is this necessary?

- Why do people feel safer in groups?

- How does God's love differ from human love?

What is God speaking to my heart?

Storm Survey
Day 17

- What is my definition of "perfect love?"

- What is my favorite promise in God's Word?

- God loves me lavishly and accepts me completely. Do I love and accept myself?

- When was the last time that I experienced childlike wonder at the greatness of God?

- Which part of the song resonated with me? Why?

What is God speaking to my heart?

Storm Survey
Day 18

- Do I struggle to make sense of my storm?

- Chains break when He is exalted! Have I ever broken into spontaneous praise during a storm?

- How does God exchange beauty for ashes?

- How would I honestly answer the questions posed in the third stanza of the poem?

- According to I Peter 4:12, why so many trials?

What is God speaking to my heart?

Storm Survey
Day 19

- What emotions do storms evoke in me?

- Have I ever wondered if the storms in my life caught The Lord by surprise?

- Is God's presence enough or do I need answers?

- Why would such a powerful God allow storms?

- What are some issues that are beyond my control?

What is God speaking to my heart?

Storm Survey
Day 20

- How do I cope with my own emotional storms?

- Am I comfortable being transparent with others?

- What emotions did Jesus experience?

- How can I support others during emotional storms?

- Is emotional pain or dysfunction caused by a lack of faith in God?

What is God speaking to my heart?

Storm Survey
Day 21

- Why are feelings so unreliable?

- When I lack clarity, what keeps me going?

- How do I know whether a storm is purposeful or simply a spiritual attack?

- According to Ephesians 6:12, who is my adversary?

- What am I doing now to strengthen my spirit?

What is God speaking to my heart?

Storm Survey Day 22

- What experiences have shaped my views on healing?

- Does fear of disappointment ever hurt my faith?

- Have I been taught that healing must be earned?

- Why do most people ignore God's prompting?

- When I read this true account, was there friction between my logical mind and my spirit?

What is God speaking to my heart?

Storm Survey
Day 23

- What does the word "family" mean to me?

- Do I have realistic expectations of others?

- Why do the people closest to us seem to push our buttons more than strangers? Explore this.

- According to the text, what are some conditions that make families more vulnerable to storms?

- What causes me to fall into the comparison trap when it comes to my own family dynamics?

What is God speaking to my heart?

Storm Survey
Day 24

- What are some of my attitudes concerning finances?

- Do I trust God when it comes to my finances?

- Are there any financial pitfalls that I can avoid?

- What is the best piece of financial advice that I ever received and how did I put this into practice?

- What promise does God make concerning my finances in Philippians 4:19?

Storm Survey
Day 25

- What is my own church background?

- What are my expectations of a local church?

- What ministry gifts do I have that could edify the local body of Christ and am I willing to use them?

- What are some valid reasons for leaving a church?

- How does church unity benefit everyone, including those outside of the church community?

What is God speaking to my heart?

Storm Survey
Day 26

- Do I ever confuse my job/career with my identity?

- If I were to grade my own response to the recent career storm, what feedback would I give myself?

- How has God designed me for maximum impact?

- What strategies has God placed on my heart for weathering this storm with His wisdom?

- What lessons have I learned through this trial and what can I do to combat my feelings of fear?

What is God speaking to my heart?

Storm Survey
Day 27

- Rejection is painful. Am I defensive towards others?

- Do I trust God enough to be authentic and vulnerable?

- What is a healthy response to abusive/toxic people?

- Am I willing to accept myself and forgive others?

- What is the difference between *constructive feedback* and *criticism* and how should I respond to each one?

What is God speaking to my heart?

Storm Survey Day 28

- On a scale of 1 to 5 (5 being the highest level), how well do I tolerate firestorms of personal attack?

- How did a *firestorm* propel Joseph to destiny?

- How can reading The Bible prepare me to weather firestorms with greater success?

- How are *reputation* and *character* different?

- After engaging in an argument, how do I feel?

What is God speaking to my heart?

Storm Survey
Day 29

- According to the song, what are the waves?

- Why is God's love compared to a hurricane?

- What does God promise to do in Jeremiah 31:4?

- What were my favorite childhood adventures?

- How can I reframe my next storm as an adventure?

What is God speaking to my heart?

Storm Survey
Day 30

- Why does the author compare *lockdown* to *hibernation*? What are my own feelings?

- What personal losses have I been grieving?

- How does Christ's death and resurrection place me in the position to conquer every storm?

- Is there anything dormant in my life that God wants to reawaken?

- Will I choose to become a S*torm Chaser*?

What is God speaking to my heart?

Storm Statements

- God is with me in this storm.

- My current storm does not dictate my destination.

- I know that this season will pass.

- God is my fortress and rock.

- I will conquer all adversity through Christ.

- My storm is purposeful.

- God is building a better version of me.

- I have God's direction and wisdom for the storm.

- One day this storm will be my victory story.

- I attract answers for every question in my storm.

- I have the favor of God on my life for this storm.

- I am open to learning something from my storm.

- If a wave knocks me down, I will rise up stronger.

- Fear will not derail God's purpose in my life.

- Added pressure only increases my value.

- God is rocking my boat to make me walk on water.

- I will prepare my heart to trust God in the storm.

- The storm clears all unwanted debris from my life.

- The worst is over and the best is yet to come.

What is God speaking to my heart?

Salvation Prayer

If you could not relate to certain content or answer all of the questions because you have never experienced salvation, you don't have to go through another storm alone. Jesus died on a cross and conquered every storm because of His limitless love.

For God so loved the world, that he gave his only
begotten Son, that whosoever believeth in him
should not perish, but have everlasting life.

—John 3:16 (KJV)—

If you are ready to accept this free gift, please pray with me:

Dear Lord, I have been trying to navigate the storms in my life without your help and guidance. I believe that you died just for me and rose from the dead; there is a purpose for my life. I need your comfort and presence now, more than ever before. I realize that you have a plan for me to conquer every storm. Please forgive me for all my sins and failures and walk beside me for the rest of my life. I surrender my life to you and exchange my confusion for completion. Jesus Christ, I accept you as my Lord and Savior, turning my back on my old life.

Thank you, Jesus, for this gift of eternal life. Through faith, I accept your unconditional love and grace to help me weather any storm. Lord, you are now my Father and I am your child. I trust your direction for my life and I ask you to be my navigator from this point forward. I choose to embrace faith instead of fear, placing my future in your capable hands. Show me who you are and what you have in store for my life. I pray this prayer in Jesus' name. Amen.

Welcome to the family. Please consider finding a church where you can continue to grow. My son (ever the philosopher) once said, "Past versions of you say nothing unless you give them a mouth." Today, I challenge you to embrace your new identity and read 2 Corinthians 5:17!

Author's Afterword

This book came into existence because I recognized a need. I had envisioned writing a book for many years, but there never seemed to be enough time. Is there ever? Then, the 2020 pandemic lockdown rocked my reverie and turned the world upside down in the blink of an eye. I realized that we were all living through a storm, yet handling our pain very differently. I kept hearing the mantra, "We are all in the same boat" and yet, that is not entirely true. We have constructed our boats very differently based on our individual fears and experiences. Some people suffer in silence and isolation while others have an enviable crisis support system.

It is my hope that this devotional will pave the way for self-exploration and deeper commitment to God. The storm survey questions located at the back of the book correspond to each day of your journey. This section is the perfect resource for group discussions, Bible studies, book clubs or individual reflection. This final step will supplement your devotions and offer further interaction with the topic and Bible passages. Although there are no pages for journaling, each topic begs the obvious question of how the reader will choose to approach the storm. I suggest that you prayerfully record your own observations and meditations after reading each daily entry. Perhaps, you may want to keep a diary or blog of your storm journey. I challenge you to invite God to speak to your heart and change you in the middle of your storm. While storms can be deafening, embrace the moments of silence; God is already there waiting.

The theme of this book is universal. Whether you are facing a literal lockdown or you feel trapped in a cycle of constant adversity, God truly understands your frustration. His Word speaks to every situation if you will just probe beneath the surface. I share from experience because I have encountered serious storms beyond the ones addressed in this book. We all have. In fact, we are in good company. Jesus encountered more storms than anyone and He overcame them all. While writing this book, I faced some new challenges that made me wonder if I had the heart to continue. Then, God used a wise person to speak these words into my life: "The worst opposition usually comes before the biggest blessing, so just keep writing that book!" Weariness fades away in the invigorating winds of God's breath when you choose to be a storm chaser.

Works Cited

"BibleGateway." BibleGateway.com: A Searchable Online Bible in over 150 Versions and 50 Languages., *www.biblegateway.com/*.

"Dictionary by Merriam-Webster: America's Most-Trusted Online Dictionary." Merriam-Webster, Merriam-Webster, *www.merriam-webster.com/*.

https://www.floridadisaster.org/globalassets/importedpdfs/damage-assessment-category-guidelines-fema-2016.pdf

Nobel, Justin. "Playing Dead For The Next Hundred Years - Hibernation Preparation Tips." Digital Dying, 25 July 2018, *www.funeralwise.com/digital-dying/playing-dead-next-hundred-years-hibernation-preparation-tips/*.

*Note: Scripture references are quoted along with each text. The Bible is public domain and each version used has been identified in parenthesis following the verse.

Works Consulted

Hancock, L., 2020. *Forest Fires: The Good And The Bad*. [online] World Wildlife Fund. Available at: <*https://www.worldwildlife.org/stories/forest-fires-the-good-and-the-bad*> [Accessed 11 May 2020].

Shaw, Ethan. "What Are Some Positive Effects of a Hurricane?" *Sciencing*, 2 Mar. 2019, *sciencing.com/positive-effects-hurricane-4462.html*.

Staff, AOS. "Fly Like an Eagle?" *American Ornithological Society*, 22 July 2019, *americanornithology.org/fly-like-an-eagle/*.

Bible Version Permission Statements

Scripture quotations marked (AMP) are taken from the AMPLIFIED® BIBLE, Copyright© 1954, 1958, 1962, 1964, 1965, 1987 by the Lockman Foundation Used by Permission. (www.Lockman.org)

The (CEB) text may be quoted up to and inclusive of five hundred (500) verses without express written permission of the publisher, provided the verses quoted do not amount to a complete book of the Bible nor account for twenty-five percent (25%) of the written text of the total work or live event in which they are quoted.

All contents of the Common English Bible Web Site are: Copyright 2012 by Common English Bible and/or its suppliers. All rights reserved.

Scripture quotations marked (CEV) are taken from the CONTEMPORARY ENGLISH VERSION, Copyright© 1995 by the American Bible Society. Used by permission.

Scripture quotations marked (ESV) are taken from THE HOLY BIBLE, ENGLISH STANDARD VERSION®, Copyright© 2001 by Crossway, a publishing ministry of Good News Publishers. Used by permission.

Scripture quotations marked (GNT) are taken from the GOOD NEWS TRANSLATION© 1994 published by the Bible Societies/ HarperCollins Publishers Ltd UK, Good News Bible© American Bible Society 1966, 1971, 1976, 1992. Used with permission.

154

About The Author

Wendy Aguiar is a middle school language arts teacher and tutor with twelve years of experience in her field. In 2016, she was honored as Teacher of the Year during a very stormy season in her life. This devotional is her first book, yet it will resonate with a wide audience for its authenticity and relevance. Wendy considers herself to be a "storm expert" based on personal encounters with storms of adversity that could have shipwrecked her life. Wendy's lifelong dream of publishing a book came to fruition when the COVID-19 pandemic prompted deep reflection. The author was recognized in 2005 by Nova Southeastern University with the distinction of Outstanding Student Graduate within the Division of Humanities. She continued working full-time and raising her son as a single parent when she returned to school, earning her master's degree in Reading Education in 2008. She contributed frequent articles to her church newsletter and currently enjoys writing songs, poetry and inspirational anecdotes. Some of her current (sans pen) hobbies include singing, sampling authentic Mexican food and shopping. Wendy resides with her family in sunny South Florida where she is adapting to the new normal of teaching online. Above all, this promising author is a Christian who believes that faith is the key to conquering every storm. She shares her spiritual insights and personal experiences in an unforgettable way. After this 30-day journey to hope, you will want to become a storm chaser!

waguiar3.wixsite.com/website
credencehousepress.com
facebook.com/wendy.aguiar.7
waguiar@mynsu.nova.edu

Made in the USA
Monee, IL
05 February 2021